ap_unwritten

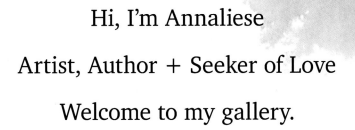

Hi, I'm Annaliese

Artist, Author + Seeker of Love

Welcome to my gallery.

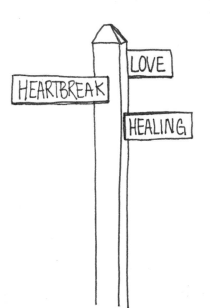

I want to welcome you into the unwritten version of my life…

You may know me as Annaliese Puccini, a cast member of
The Bachelor and Bachelor In Paradise.

Or, maybe you've never heard of me until today.

Somewhere in between the infamy I've struggled through and the
anonymity I crave is where this journal begins.

I am unwinding what the world knows of me and what it thinks of me,
writing a new path for myself. I'm unpacking my patterns, and habits –
my old ideas of love and how it's "supposed" to work out, and writing a
new chapter for myself and for all of you …

For most of my life, I have been running on a hamster wheel, finding
myself in the same rock-bottom place. Over and over again - especially
when it comes to love, going around and around with the same results,
"why does this keep happening to me?"

Break-up after break-up, heartbreak after heartbreak, both privately and
very publicly, I kept finding myself on the wrong side of heartache.

I would simply hope and wish that a new partner would "complete me" and bring new energy. That "this time it would be different". But it wasn't, because I never did the deep healing or reflection I needed. I would try to manage my emotions in the "acceptable" way, the "grown-up" way, the "as-seen-on-TV" way. I would look for hope, wisdom, advice and healing by hitting pause on dating, working on myself and then undoubtedly running into the arms of another man … and never fully letting myself be enough.

After another devastating relationship blow, I needed a change! I decided that it was time to get off the wheel, time to end the patterns I had learned over the years, and break the cycle of heartbreak, loneliness and despair. Finally, I decided to do it another way and figure out my way.

During difficult times I would turn to therapy, podcasts, reinvesting in myself and I would look to my bookshelf.

The problem is: my brain processes information differently than most people — a result of neurodiversity (learning differences) I discovered when I was a child — so, I found it hard to process words I was reading about relationship advice I so desperately wanted. Reading, writing or even listening for too long would exhaust me. It wouldn't stick, especially if I wasn't in a space to actively receive.

As a result, I often felt alone in my healing.

Lots of effort with little results.
This book was born from my own breaking point:
the moment I realized that we can't change if nothing
changes. If what I was doing wasn't working I needed
to find what worked for me.

If you truly want to end a cycle you need
to heal the root of this cycle or else you
will keep repeating it.

But I'm not here to tell you how to do that;
Rather, I want to inspire you to rewrite your own
story, retell your own truth … do it your own way.

My way: through art and spoken word.

I realized that I often view life as part of a little
art installation.

Annaliese on art:
Creating
Taking thoughts and making them into something.
It's unique and an insight into how we see the world.
Bright colors or dark and moody
Complicated or simply minimalistic.
Putting things together only your brain can see possible.
Art is therapy, getting your inner visions, thoughts, feelings out.
In this journal, you will see inside my brain and into my own art
installation – a journey through love, heartbreak and healing.

My thoughts are choppy at times and I often think in spoken word,
rather than traditional storytelling.

Offering you a chance to participate: However you process information
is beautiful and hopefully one of these visual tools will resonate with you.

On your journey and your space to get and take whatever you need
from this book, finding your words, images, thoughts, passions.

Whatever to help you turn the page and step out of the cycle and onto a new path.

Right along with me. *Annaliese*

OPENING

I don't remember the exact moment I knew I was different.

It wasn't as if something just clicked. Actually quite the opposite,
things I was told "should" click, didn't.

It was always just me. Who I was.

A hopeful believer that all people were good.

A lover of love. An artist.

A dreamer.

It was maybe somewhere between fourth and fifth grade.

Between trying so hard and being so soft.

Between mostly getting things wrong and almost never feeling right.

It was around this time I noticed my grades were the lowest
and my fears were the highest.

I struggled when teachers would call on me for fear I'd embarrass myself.

Answer a question. Read aloud.

Both I'd surely mess up.

In front of everyone.

I excelled in only two subjects: art and physical education.

The ones that never seemed "to matter". Where books were not needed.

For the rest, I studied hard.

For weeks and days leading up to each test.

When my friends were out playing, barely flipping a chapter
or a page and doing just fine.

I would fight to memorize. To understand.

Comparison slowly becoming my biggest challenge.

Why didn't it stick for me? Why do I study so hard and still fail?

The not being good enough, or as good as my peers, I just began to accept.

All the times I fell in love too hard.

And was hardly understood.

What a gift it would have been to simply understand
what I was doing wrong.

Or whether I could ever be right.

And then came the diagnosis. A window into me.

Maybe I wasn't just the dumb blonde, whose body developed
earlier than her confidence.

Maybe I simply processed differently.

Maybe it wasn't me who needed to change how I was learning,

But the learning that needed to change how it was speaking.

Do all pages need completion? I questioned.

Do all sentences need to look the same? I wondered.

What does the empty space say? Does it speak?

Can art and movement tell stories, too?

I imagined what it would be like if books were more like art museums:

With exhibitions and installations and galleries and blank walls.

With room to walk through and turn around.

With room to sit down, to observe.

For visiting, revisiting, exploring, thinking, painting, drawing, imagining.

Inspiring your own art.

Rewriting.

Un-writing.

This was my motivation then. And it remains my motivation now:

To inquire. To dig deeper. To be curious. To be my best.

Not your best. My best.

To un-write the written. To re-write my beliefs. To make art.

To find love (for me and in everything).

To find me.

This is my art journal, but I want you to make it your own. If you feel inspired to draw or write I encourage you to doodle next to my drawings and make this our collaborative art and poetry journal! Please share your art and poetry by tagging ap_unwritten, I can't wait to see your creations!

EXHIBITION
love

Life is better
With you
But that much you knew

Something where there wasn't supposed to be
Not looking for connection
When you least expect life's lessons
Blessings beckoning
They show up, often unwanted but necessary
An understanding stranger
She was vulnerable and raw
He was kind and thoughtful
And just like that she was in awe
An unexpected connection
Where energy was exchanged
He was no longer a stranger
There was a gentle tenderness to his soul
That soothed and excited her
It was simple he held her, stroked her softly and showered
her with kindness...
And, in that moment, that was all she needed

pick 3 words and write. My poem was built from

connection, simple, soft

Connection in the direction of two souls
Pulled to be
A feeling of how do they know me?
Are we a we?
A vibe a tribe?
People brought together
Bridging the gap
Between unknown and knowing
A spark
A light
A thought
A connection can literally ignite from unclear sight

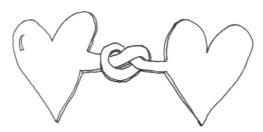

Where to even start
The way to my
Heart
Is in art
Through your words
The feelings grew
Painting a picture
Overdue
Drawn in by what I knew
Excited for the new
The images you drew
To songs I knew
That made me think of you
As I continue to get to know
You

draw a heart inspired by a song

Slow down
Pump the breaks
Things are moving along
At an alarming rate
Take time to evaluate
You must walk
Before you run
So take a stroll
And
Take it slow
This is not a race
Just a date
With my soul mate

The road is long
Just like the song
We sang
Along
That moved
Through
And made me move to
The rhythm of the sun
That moved you
As the light
Vibrated
Through

We knew truth
The journey
Wrote the song
And so we sang along
Rose colored glasses
Made me sing along
Never realizing
The words were all wrong
But we danced and basked
Because we didn't care
If our love was wrong

Feeling the beat
Of the rhythm
Of my heart
As it moves through
The short
Intake
A quick take
Without mistake
A smooth
Beat break
Closing in on my
Breath
As I take in another inhale
Not to derail
Only to exhale

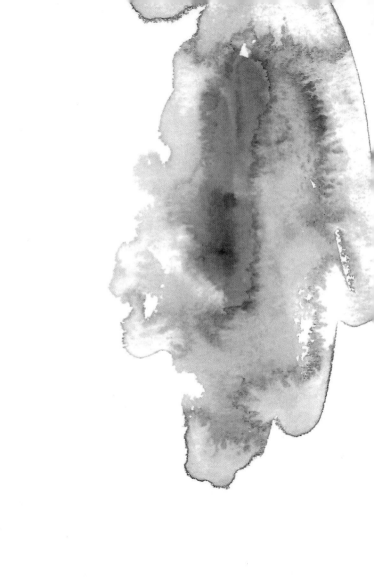

I think I always knew it was you
From that night
I looked at you
From across the room
You were probably doing
something stupid
But I thought to myself
That's the man I'm going to spend
my life with No hesitation
No doubt
Absolute certainty
It was you

I didn't laugh
Or smile
Or even move
I just sat there
So still
So sure
As someone telling me the sky is blue
Sitting in truth
Of how I felt for you
Calm
And
Home
No weak knees
Just a happy girl
Pleased

What do you feel when you read this? Does it make you think of a time you were in love? Content? Happy? Calm?

Your heart it intertwined
With mine
Like fine wine
You must drink it at the right time
But with us
There was so much time
And our time was always
Quite fine
But too fast
And too much
Is not a good sign
Your belly will hurt and your heart will ache
And you'll need to stop and take a break
For too much wine can be divine
Too much wine can be just fine
But too much
Too much
There is no such thing
When it comes to us

Daydream believer
The mystery and wonder
That struck me
With awe
The daydreamer
Awake with hope
Restless in the picture painted
So excited to awake
But blissfully content in the dream

Let yourself daydream and write or draw about where your mind wanders off to...

The last thing I read

Was
Go to bed
Too tired to comprehend
The dreams swirling
Around in my head
So I left you on read
As my eyes grew heavy
And I drifted
To bed
Dreaming of
What dreams may come ahead

In my head
In my bed
With messages … unsaid

Magic and light
Something bright
A road map to find you at midnight
To kiss you under the moonlight
Our hearts igniting in the night

It all happened in a blink of an eye
The connection
Between you and I
The very thing that crossed
My mind
Was
Take your time
This time
A lot's at stake
And your heart could ache

If you don't take your time
Destined and fate
And divine time
To lose your mind
Lose sight
Just in time
Wait and anticipate
What's meant
Cannot break
So take your time
Avoid and alleviate
The pain and divide
Of what's yours and mine
Take your time
And you'll be just fine

The work is never done
But I choose you
Today and everyday
To grow with you along the way
Through whatever challenges are thrown our way
Nothing is standing in our way
We have been to hell and back
And now we know our strength
Our fight
And what skills will get us through
I wish you only knew
How much I cherish you

Your blessings will come
When the time is right
Even if they seem out of sight
Or when love feels like a constant fight
An uphill battle
There is no right
Or wrong day
Your gut and soul will lead the way

Have faith our hearts
Will know the way

For every set back
Is a way
To loving you each and every day

No stopping us
We have mountains to climb
Adventures to amend
This is not the end
Just the start
For the next time we meet
We will know
This is the plan
Because I chose you
And I hope you understand
That we can weather any storm
And not just lay in the sand

use an adventure to inspire a poem

I know this time
That for the 1st time
I choose me 1st
And you are not mine
Just two people whole
Intertwined
Not letting go this time

This kind of love
Surely
Is hard to find

Hot summer nights
Had me ready to delight
In endless
Ice cream
But those nights are drawing
To a close
Hot summer nights
Will now
Not be so close
As fall sets
Snow cones
To snow falls
As snow flakes
Kiss my nose
You hold me tight
Through the winter night
Warm with delight

EXHIBITION

heartbreak

In an instance you were gone
And I was wrong
To ever let you into
The part of my heart that
Wrote a love song

This is one goodbye I thought I'd never say
Please don't go away
I will not beg
I will let you go your way
That's for you to say
You go or stay
If you want to stay
That choice is yours today
And everyday

I will cry
There's no other way
My heart never thought you'd walk away
But that's not fair for me to say
There were probably signs along the way

All the good made me blind
The bad hard to find

2 people in love
But needed more

There was much more there to explore
That's for sure
But inside each of us
Something was crushed
The problem was not us
The problem was within us
Both issues to resolve

Alone
And get back to whole on our own

how are you breaking free from the mold?

Belittle me
Like you mold me out of clay
Chipping away
Making me feel smaller
Everyday

Broken like a rubber band
Snapped from hand to hand
Juggling the idea that has been written in sand
Of who I am

2 days
Just blew
Up in my face
My world turned upside down
Inside out
And fell to the ground
My tower came crashing
Crumbling down
I had no clue
That you
Would be the one to knock me down
But you
You were my safe space
My home
And just like that

Something had overgrown
Strangling us
Pushing me to the ground
Kicking dirt in my face
I could not face
My new reality
There was no trace
Of you and me
Only memories
You could not face
Full of disgrace
Just trying now to save face
Put a smile on my face
And face a face, I can face

He scared her sometimes
She thought
He might hurt her heart
Or body with a mark
A bite or a bruise
Is how he left his mark
When they were together in the dark
With little threatening remarks
Darts through her heart
He drew his dagger
She never knew
If this one would pierce all the way through

Her fear grew
And when she spoke her truth
He withdrew
The relationship doomed
But her heart
It grew
And she knew
She spoke her truth
Protected her heart
And it was ok that this relationship
Went dark

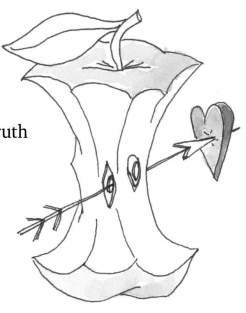

Shhh
Gushing along
Drowning any other sound
Streaming along
Calming at times
But with
A rush and a gush
A ferocious wet thunder
Taking what's yours and mine
Carving a way
Through the hardest stones
Never stopping for anyone
Or anything

No agenda
But to flow
Watermarked by every current
Every gush
Every rush
You get to where you are going
Going with the flow
Not overthinking for a moment
Just being
All alone

As silence becomes all we know

Sick to my stomach
Over you
I cannot eat
I'm so overdue
For a feast
And to get over you

draw your feast

It should've been the happiest
Instead it was the saddest
Maddest
The life I thought I knew
That the universe disapproved
Moving me away from you
The destruction
The confusion
You put me through
No apology
Of the hurt
Pushed by you
The only way to move
On from you
Is to accept
This was not on me
Forgiveness through
Accepting
This was actually always you

what would you call this chapter of your life?

Wait or evaluate
The corners of my mind

Don't say I never tried
I tried all the time
But my time was not enough
You weren't ready for you and I
Perfect can be scary
Could we be this good all the time?
Was a concept you weren't quite ready
To accept for you and I

I wanted to melt
But all I felt
Was don't fall to the floor
The more I wept
The thought crept
Into your mind

That maybe
Never mind
I feel what you feel
But can't show it all the time
The way you look is how I feel
Just only worse
Is my state of mind
But those are the cards I dealt myself
Ridiculous thoughts running through my mind
Taking over what was fine
Walking away from what was mine
Commitment strangling me alive
Turning away from you because I'm blind
I'm so scared I cannot look at you this time
Closing myself off is something I thought I'd never do
Ignoring what could be with you

Knock me down
To see me fall
But what happens when I get back up
And stand OH so tall
Growing everyday
Looking for new ways
To make my mark on this world
Not failing today
There is no way
I'll prove you wrong
The right way
By working hard
For you are wrong in every way
I am stronger everyday
Finding my way
My back is NOT up against a wall
I am free to make a change
To be brave and walk away
And find my way

My drive is there
No question there
I just need some air
To breathe in change
And get somewhere

Trust
Fixing me is a must
I'll soon come out of the dust

But life without you
Is something new
I must get used to

And just like that
You were gone
A long goodbye
That made me cry
But not goodbye
A see you soon
Standing there
Wrapped in your arms
So tight
Not wanting to let go
But our bags are packed
For a journey

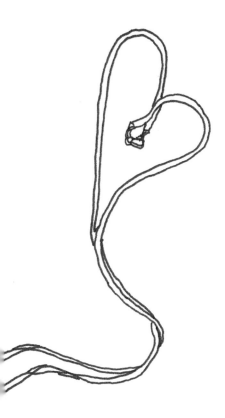

Different and yet the same
The plane will leave
And I'll meet you there
This journey may be long so don't delay
No time to play

Not today
But I will see you soon
Hope that's still ok
Once we've done the work
On an island full of growth
Lush and full of hope
If that day is the day to run
away and play like we did
yesterday

Then I look forward to that day

Cause, I don't want to ever say
Please go away

All the good memories
Can not fade away
They can not fly away
There is never going to be a day
Where our time gets turned away
Do the work
I'll say
To myself
Otherwise there is no, hey
There is no bae

So judged
But it's part of my DNA
Engraved in every way
Deep down to my core
In my every groove
I try to fight it but what's the use
You'll find it and use
It to abuse
Your judgment of me
Is the only thing that you'll see
Deny what is me
For you to accept all

That YOU want me to be
But that's not ME
That's not me
I'm not what you want me to be
Who you think I should be
Or live up to that ONE thing
That you now hold over me
Just let me be
Let me be me
And please don't judge
I'm done defending me

It's not ok
To put a
Bandaid
On your pain
To try to make it
Go away
A bandaid
Will not heal
Where you need to grow
It will cover up the story that's meant to show
That will unfold
In your mind

If you just give it time
To heal
If you don't cover up
What is real
The pain will
Be unreal
But you need that pain
To heal
Let's be real

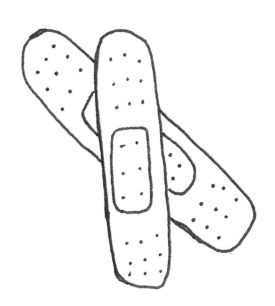

The more you run
The faster they come
And catch up with you
You eventually need
To overcome
The pain that scares you
And makes you run
Stop
Running from
What you've already done
Or else you'll prevent
Beautiful things
That are sure to come

usée
l'imprimerie
de la communication
raphique

I'm not lonely
But trying to figure out
If I still miss you
Working out any doubt
In my mind
And body
To embody
The part of me that feels left behind
Without you

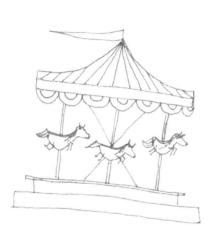

around we go

Get a grip
A grip…
While I let go
Here we go
On 2 separate paths
Finding our own
MO
2 trains
One ready to go
The other circling
Like a
Merry go-
Round and round you go
While I flow

In a new direction
Direct
Speeding up
And not looking back
You'd better get off that track
Round and round
And find new ground
To move forward
To catch up
To find your way back
To grip
Onto
Ohhh
Now I get why you had to let go
Of that grip...ohhh

Your mask
Makes me sad
It's not you at all
It's you avoiding
That's all
Too scared to fall
Running from
It all

What mask do you hide behind?

Not a man of your word
Or so I've heard
Making promises
That you'll never keep
Just to keep
The peace
To run from
What's to come
Always
On the run from
Who you might become
So you hurt people along the way
To get your way
To never give up
A Peter Pan life

And push away
Anything that could get in the way
But it's the lies you choose
To live your life from
It's the lies
You abuse
To get life from
And it's the lies that will make you lose
Out on a life
You could get from
Everything you've hid from
And been on the run from
Be a man of your word

It's absurd

I always hated when you lied
Just to get by
Selfishly
Doing what you please
Only to appease
The stories you've written
Of more "interesting" scenes
You're full of these
Lies
Roping me in
To justify
The images
Of reality

That only you can see

write using a vice as inspiration

draw a self portrait

Scared of yourself
Scared to look in the mirror
At what you'll see
Scared to find out
WHO
You might actually be
The demons
Will be set free
And you'll see what you
Don't want to see
Faced with anything
And everything
Is a scary thing
Scared to death
Of what you might really be
So instead you fill
Your life
To fill the void
So you can avoid
Setting your demons free

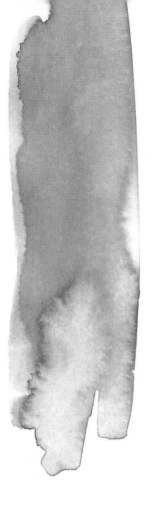

You need to be alone
Fight this battle on your own
Trepidation
Till you've grown

Just like a hurricane
It blew through us with a gusto
A gust of wind so strong and powerful
We couldn't brace

Winds whipping
Cutting through every space

A storm we couldn't escape
Much to replace
Lost in thin air
Understand that some things
We're unable to repair

Numb
Is a way
To save the pain
For another day
When you can no longer hide away
And the pain will sneak up
And fill you with rain
Stale and old
And even cold
At your core
Frozen
In pain
Numb
Feels like the only way
To salvage the day
Push these feelings away
Deep down
So that they can erupt
Another day

Deep breath
In … out
In … out
Let it in
Let it go
Repeat what we know

Life
Love
None the same
No breathe the same
All unique
Yet we try to repeat what we know
You are my favorite
Yet drive me wild
Even mad at times
You make me tingle
Testing every bit of me

With every bite and every thought
With every breathe
Every word
Every touch
My heart beats
My body shakes
My brain thinks
It thinks
And it thinks
I think too much
Just be in the moment, I think
Taking me out of the moment to think
Just feel I think
I feel …
I think ?
I think or do I know
Am I curious to grow
Or am I scared of what I may show
If I think, I can control

If I let go
Then here we go

It's a cliff
Do I fall
Let go
See where this goes
Release the ropes
and lose control
Trust the fall
On my own
Heart beating
Alive

Grateful
For you
For me
For this ...
All of this

The falls
The mess
The growth
Not solely on my own
Together
We do not crawl
No
We climb
To the tallest mountain
And if we fall only we will know
For the fall is where we grow
And we repeat what we know

So let go

When a heart breaks
The earth quakes
Inviting sadness and darkness
There is no saving grace
It takes
And takes
And what's lost feels as if
It can not be replaced
Out of place in this world
Drifting through space
Lost

So let me plant a seed of hope
To get you to see growth
This is not the end
This is where we begin
To find our place
In this world you can not be replaced
So be grateful for what got you to this place

heavy heart

Look for the light
Even in the darkness of the night
It's cliche but that's alright
We go through it all
The good, the bad and sometimes we fall
Hard
And break
Rock bottom some might say
Think
But don't overthink
Get back up and rethink
Life can change
But so can we
No reason to stay

Never growing from our falls
Let life replace
What keeps us
In one place

Move forward and face the light
It will only help you to ignite
The questions you fear
Become clear
Look to the light
It's cheesy but it's bright
And that's you
Getting through

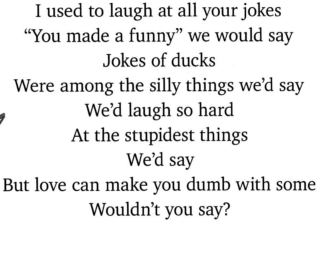

I used to laugh at all your jokes
"You made a funny" we would say
Jokes of ducks
Were among the silly things we'd say
We'd laugh so hard
At the stupidest things
We'd say
But love can make you dumb with some
Wouldn't you say?

Home
It didn't feel like much
Empty inside
Alone
With too much time on my side
To make this house a home

Tied with pain
But nothing to gain
If this time was in vain
I'd go insane
So I'll do the work
This time with no one to blame

But myself
Since all I had was time and pain
In this house
Cold and full of distain
A sign came just in time
A rainbow appeared
Took away some of my fears
A rush came over me
A cry
A sigh
That some day
I'll understand why all these tears had to be cried

A pandemic
In us all
A virus
Putting up walls
Only phone calls
From bathroom walls
Dating these days
From inside our walls

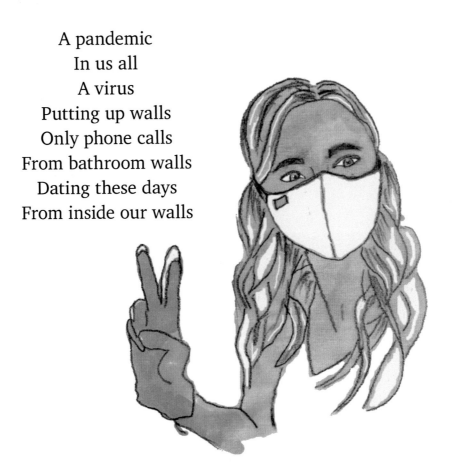

Mindfulness
More like
Mind full
Of a mess
Yeah…
For someone full of mindfulness
You sure are kind of a mess
Not using your mind
Not kind
And yes
A mess
Mind full
But full
Of what?

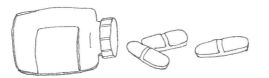

You want to go away
But you can't stay away
Like a drug
Again and again
You come back to play
And let that mess get in the way
Filling up with
Vices and vices
To fill any gap
Of the indecisive
Pieces of your mind
That are ready
To let go of the mess
And finally
Get on top of the mindfulness

Home is where the heart is
But if my heart is with you
I am homeless
Lost without your love

So I'll start building my own home
Finding me without you

What's done is what's been done
The writing is on the wall
That someday you will call
Too late
To even crawl
Back to me at all

What a journey it will be
To discover what's meant for
Me
Not you and me
Of course that still could be
But this journey is just for me
Sorry that's what needs to be
For now
I need to find the how
The why
The who
I'm meant to be
To be proud of all I could be

In every way
For this is for me
Today and everyday
I need to grow
That's for me to know
And how
I will show
But this is not for you
Although you could help me through
You've been here too
To start anew
Another chapter
Where you'll look back on

And think
"Man I grew"
If you only knew
How hard this is
To walk away
To work on me
Excited
Scared
Hurting still
In every way
I know the time will come
When I can finally say
Thank you
For the space to face
Another day
And find me
Along the way

Destructive
To everything in your way
Hurting me
While punishing you
So you stand in your own way
Trying to get in the way
Pushing a good thing down
Before it can get you down
Falling in love
And then avoiding the fall
Doing your best to avoid it all
Even when destiny calls

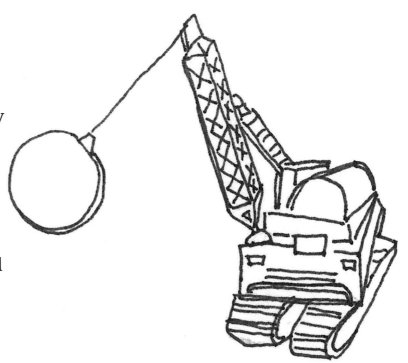

Gut punch
And just like that I'm liquified
Tears falling from my eyes
This is the last goodbye

I'm done
I'm done with love
I'm done with you
For all you do
Is pull back
Dude your reasonings are wack
And now you're making me look back
On what felt like a heart attack
I'm not going back
No more love
That shits like crack

I'm addicted
To this drug
That pulls me back
But every time leaves me flat
On my back
On the floor
And now I'm floored
And I can't take this anymore
So I'm done with love
Until it's ready to give back
And take back all the heart attacks

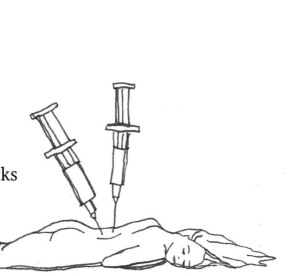

You used to breathe me in
Like I was the only air you needed
Deep
Full breaths
Sucking the air from me
So you could get even closer
Inside me
Inviting me into your body
Into your air
It was never enough
I was the oxygen
That filled you up
With love
With laughter

And sometimes even pain
Yearning for the air
I breathed
To become your air
To fill yourself with my joy
My love
My light
I had no doubts that
You breathed new life into me
Sucking away any stale air
That pain was blocking me
You brought life into me
Oxygenated me
We breathed each other in

Like there was no hope
For any other air
To fill the air
You gave me hope
You gave me light
You gave me tears
Now, Wipe away these fears of losing you
Renew my breath
And give me hope once more
Take away this pain
Of suffocating
Without your air
My lungs are bare

EXHIBITION

healing

As a girl
She had dreams of what she'd be
Ambitious and driven
A student
A wife
A mother
Dreams for a life she had no clue about
What was meant to be
Her destiny
A life she thought she knew
All written out
Waiting for it to happen
But woke up one day to find that girl
Had gone away
No sight of her anywhere
She disappeared
With all the hopes and dreams
She had planned away
Just drifting through life
Hoping for a better day
With no plan or purpose

She could not find her way
Losing the best things to ever come her way
Getting off her ass to find her way

Wipe the slate clean of what could have been
Close the chapter and start anew again
New purpose
New ambitions

No holding on
To what went "wrong"
This time she would let go and move on

Building blocks
That no wolf could blow down
She would be strong in her fortress
The queen of her castle
Nothing could take her down
Everything up until now
Had knocked her down

Done feeling sorry for herself
Done living in the past
It's time to step away
Come what may
But do the work
And still find time to play
Your life is yours
Today and everyday
That girl is me
And I am on my way
Nothing written in pen
This is not the end
Nothing to be erased
Only embraced

use a dream to inspire a poem

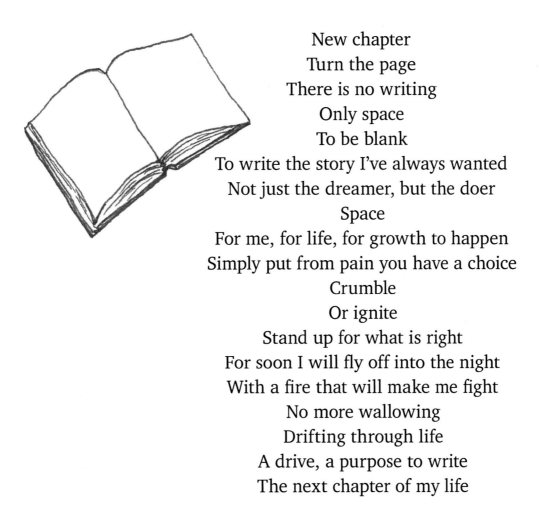

New chapter
Turn the page
There is no writing
Only space
To be blank
To write the story I've always wanted
Not just the dreamer, but the doer
Space
For me, for life, for growth to happen
Simply put from pain you have a choice
Crumble
Or ignite
Stand up for what is right
For soon I will fly off into the night
With a fire that will make me fight
No more wallowing
Drifting through life
A drive, a purpose to write
The next chapter of my life

The pain behind those teary eyes
Nothing to disguise
The pain it overwhelms
And your face paints a picture of your insides
Fighting not to cry
Heavy all the time
The pain will not go away
Feeling grey all day
Everyday
Until one day
You wake up and the pain has started to melt away
Your teary eyes will dry up
And little by little
You'll rise up
Until you realize times up
And step up to a better day

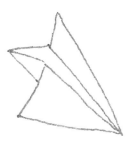

write a poem using travel as inspo

On a plane again
I've been here before
Opening a door
Embarking on a new journey
I've never seen before
New questions
New fears
And different tears
So scared
And trying to be brave
Butterflies in my chest
My stomach in knots

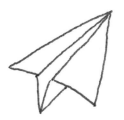

There is no turning back now
But somehow
I will figure it all out
Without any doubt
Because I know
It's time to grow
To go
On my own
With a leap of faith
Here I go

draw your heart being filled up

Heart broken
But heart awoken
Time for healing
I know this feeling
From hurt before

Deep diving
Into a sea of emotions
I've never known
Exploring the depths
Out of the shallows
Finding my fins
Diving deeper and deeper
Getting darker and darker
Moving from the surface
Knowing how to find my breath

My way back up

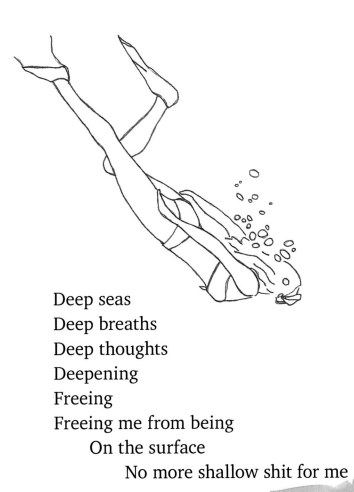

Deep seas
Deep breaths
Deep thoughts
Deepening
Freeing
Freeing me from being
    On the surface
        No more shallow shit for me

New me
Flourishing
Determined
Believing no longer
In what used to be
Moving on from a path I thought I'd be
On...
But stopped
Took time to grow
So I could sew
Lit-er-ally

Stitching my world back together
Fig-ur-a-tive-ly

Who determines your worth? I used to feel worth from other's opinions of me but the only person who actually determines your worth is .. YOU

It wasn't an island

But she felt all alone
In a vast body of water
Standing on her own
Alone she felt
Surrounded she wept

But she was not alone at all

Still feeling sad, she knew
What many were going through
On their own island
So she grew

draw an island

She grew strong
And knocked down walls
She reached out a hand
Neighbors and communities did too
We became stronger together
Standing tall on our islands
Till the day
Would come

To look back at what's been overcome

Alone alas
Do I feel free you ask
More space
And time
To be free
Of any mask
The oxygen all me
Quietly to be me
Assessing on my own
Silence enmeshing
To a new degree
In new thoughts
That are all me
New talks

Of
How to be
Set free
Breaking cycles
Of how it used to be
Ready to move on
From the recycled thoughts
I'm setting free
Letting be
Wings guiding me
To the place I'm meant to be
Independent and set free
No clipping me of what I'm meant to be
My wings will set me free

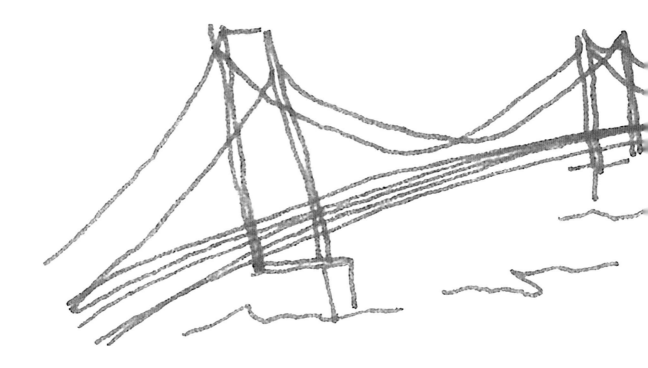

Crossing bridges
One step at a time
Don't worry you'll be fine
Keep your head up
Move forward
You'll get there just fine
One step at a time
Don't rush to the other side
The journey is all part of the ride

draw where your journey will lead you

Learning to begin again
But where to even start
What will be the end
A daunting thought
But with one step
You begin
Your journey in
Down a road
Where you do not know
The end
Only to begin
Again

No more tears to cry
I need to pick myself up
Or else I will surely die
Of pain and heartbreak
Of losing sight
Of who am I
Done with feeling this way
This place I know too well
This feeling is not invited to stay
Depressed
Hurt
My heart battered and bruised
I can not be here again
I will never be here again
This pain is not my friend
It's no longer welcomed in
It can't get in
I'm fighting
Cause I fear
I have no choice here
It's do or die

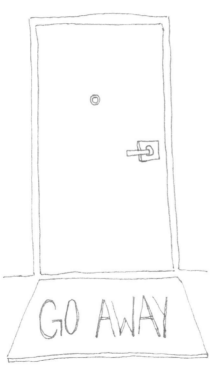

GO AWAY

This time I choose
To try
To build a stronger me
Someone who can not easily break
And who will no longer take
This kind of heart-break
My heart can't handle another break
So I'm focusing on me
And only me
On healing me
This will be a new side to me
A friend I'll gladly see
A beginning of a stronger me

create an affirmation and use it as the title for a poem

Left behind
Out alone in the cold
But was willing to be so bold
And make a change from the story
I've been told
Not letting the cold
Get in
Instead
Looking at what's within
Inside of me
You see
There is no fear stopping me
Doubting me
The only doubt in me
Is not truly loving me
And that can not be..

You may have left
But what's in front of me
Is truly what is meant to be
I will finally see
My destiny
Is
The love
I have for me

Sometimes pain
Is what you need to gain
To understand
The lessons there
Clouded in what could have been
What might have been
No pain
No gain
Is what they say

But gaining strength along the way

No longer letting rose colored glasses guide my way

I'm on my own journey
Finding
ME … now
What's important
To me
Anyhow?

Questions
That have been buried in me
Deep down
Stop running from these questions
And answer me now
Facing these questions
And finding me somehow
Answering these questions
I thought would scare me now
Sad
Judged
Crying out that's not me
Now

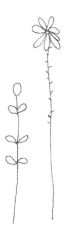
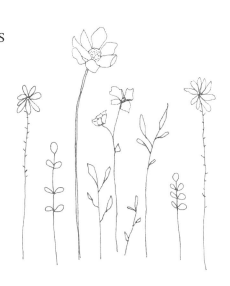

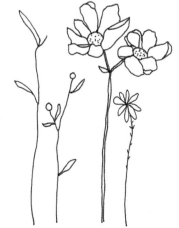

What are lies you've held onto that you've told yourself?

what's important to you?

Where your focus goes
Energy flows
Like a river
Emotions flow
Focus your energy on you

Where your focus goes
Your energy flows
Flowing back to you

Be open to the change
Let the unknown
Choose you

What's meant for you will always find a way
Do not run or hide
Let life play out this way
For this plan is for you
Today and every day

It was written for you before you could even choose
It anyways…

The walls closing in
Or expanding out
We see what we want to see
What we need to see
Bricks
Walls of a chimney
Climbing high
Balance to brace
Not to fall
A sliver in the sky
Narrow to the eye
Squeezing through
The risk
The reward
The challenge
Of rising way up high
And at the top
We will find
It's worth the wild ride
Reward is in the climb

Don't miss out on what might have been
Living in what should have been
What could have been
What's new?...
again...

We learn from
The ones that hurt us the most
The ones
That become ghosts
That take us out of a life
Where we just coast
Because
The ones that hurt us
The most
Break us down
To the ground
To rebuild
On a new foundation
With new strength and determination

Using nature to heal,
grounded, rooted, connected...

Healing yourself through mother nature, clearing away
blockages and cobwebs to see clearly.

Appreciating the little things, a snow flake, a petal, a sunrise that dazzles your eyes and
makes you realize beauty in
everything... including yourself.

I want you to focus on a star, a plant, a sunset, or put your feet in the sand, snow or dirt
... to connect with the earth.

Then use your inspiration to move you to a mood or a feeling.
If a tear runs down your face, let it. If you feel a warm glow
from within, embrace it. If you start to smile, dig deep
to make that smile wider.

Using nature to heal pain, is one of my favorite ways to feel like myself again and have
gratitude, for things "bigger" than me.

Feel to heal.

Just a prick
A thorn
Hardened to the world
Protecting … what is
Life
Resilience
Weathering the elements
Getting through
When the tough gets tough
We get tough
To protect
What is
The reason we stand
The reason we fall
The reason for it all

Grounded
Rooted in me
My feet under me
Feeling the earth
Really feeling me
Self reflection
Introspection
Is the journey I am on
Leading me
Taking steps
To finding
The real me
The me I lost
And long to be
Giving me new life
Nurturing me
Feeding me
New air

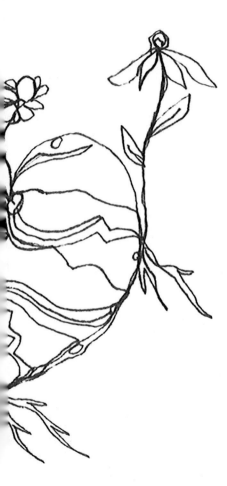

To clear the air
Refreshing breaths
Fill my lungs
Refreshing me from the musk
That filled the air with dust
Drowned me
Silenced me
Taking my air
My every breath
But life has given me
A gift
To breath again
New deep air filling me
Planting me in reality
Grounding me
In the endless possibilities
Of who I'm meant to be

Create the life
The picture you want to see
Changing focus
Changing seasons
Watch the colors of the leaves
Wait for
The light to change
The scenes to exchange
And rearrange
The focus of what's in frame

Run around the sun
This one not so fun
But grateful for what I've done
The ups were tons of fun and filled with love
But the downs helped me to realize
Who I've become and the strength
From which I have
Overcome
Ending a cycle
Finally
Getting off the tricycle
Finally
I've learned some major lessons
Finally
Freeing myself to move forward
Breaking free

Freeing me
Of the judgments of who I should be
Allowing me
To move direct
On my track
A bullet train
No stopping me
No looking back
Grateful for life
And another opportunity
To move forward
Break the mold
And start a new year
In my true authenticity

when you think of the sea what do you see?

See
What I see
Here
Are waves
Of a sea
I dare, go near
Without complete fear
Only respect
And prayers here
For an ocean
I'm drawn to be
Near

Waves of moods
Of the blues
The highs and lows
And thoughts of you
Wash
No not just wash
Crash
Crash into me like a ton of bricks
Fine
And then crash
The water flows inside
Then comes out
Like an ocean flowing from within
Uncomfortably
Filling my day with just me
No distractions
Looking at my reflection
I don't always like what I see
Tears flowing from my eyes

I suddenly snap back
To me
To fine
Even thriving at times

what's your favorite season?

Tides changing
Just like the seasons
Come and go
So does it flow
New waves
Kissing and misting the air
That is growing brisker
Sandy toes
Falling snow on your nose
A leaf falls
As fall calls
Tides rolling in
Calling you to go within
Warm your heart
Is an art
We can all learn
To love again

Pastel skies
Glimmering in my eyes
Violet, blushing on the rise
As the sun sets
On another day
We look on
And say
I'm grateful for
The dreams
That come my way...

As night falls
And dreams call
The violet sky
Turns to grey
The sun begins to fade away
And a twinkle
Gives us hope
For another day

Seeding a change
Planted in me
Nestled in my heart
Is where it ought to be

Leaves of change
Will come my way
Changing the seasons
As leaves fall away
The orange sets in
The chill in the air
Blows in
Settling in
A season of change
Will now begin
Focusing on how
To find growth from within
Just as the earth
Too

Is settling in
To this new season
New chapter
New growth
To begin
Change
Has found a friend
To wrap up in
As the leaves change
And begin to fall

Release the fall
And fall...again

The sun came up
And so did I
To face the blue sky
Of another day
Warm
And fresh
A reset
A rebirth in a way
New possibilities
Endless opportunities
A chance to clear away
The cobwebs
Breathe in life
Get excited for what's to come
Move past from what's been done
Living in the present
Today is the day
Gifts will come my way

Sun rising
No surprising
Every day
A new chance
To seize the day
More to give away
And take away
To step away
With another take away
Learning every day
Beginnings
Of what may come my way

without judgment of your 1st thought write a poem
with the sun as your inspiration

Follow the star
From where you are
That shines bright
To get you through
To guide you to
The star of wisdom
Full of truth
Lighting up
A dark sky
To shine a light
To enlighten you

The stars
They felt so bright
Like I could reach up and hold one tight
To my chest
Pulling light into my heart
In the dark
Waiting for the cold air
To warm as the sun rises
Healing
Cleansing
Energizes
Heart chakra
Open to
Abundant love
Filling up
My heart
Just like
The stars
Never giving up
Lighting up
My heart will never give up

Thankful
And oh so grateful
She thought of her world
And although
Her journey had been rocky
She thought of all the blessings
And in a quick moment
Her vibration
Made a shift
So much to be grateful for
Laughter and love
Divine guidance from above
Grateful for the good, the bad
Both beautiful
With many lessons
Her gratitude overflowing
With a new attitude
She inspired others
To shift too
All around her
A higher vibration grew

write a gratitude list and turn it into a poem

She focused on the pain
Not realizing all that's been gained
In a momentary refrain
Coming out of the rain
She flew out of the shadow
Her wings brand new
Emerging from her cocoon
As the butterfly she always knew

Thank you for joining me through a
collection of my
words and illustrations.
I would love to see and share
your poems and drawings.
Please share them with #ap_unwritten

♡, *Annaliese*

Design and Artwork by Annaliese Puccini
Book Layout by Electra Design Group
Edited by Annaliese Puccini
Publishing Support | TSPA The Self Publishing Agency, Inc.

Made in the USA
Las Vegas, NV
23 February 2022